WHITEOUT

WHITEOUT

JESSICA GOODFELLOW

Published by
University of Alaska Press
P.O. Box 756240
Fairbanks, AK 99775-6240

Cover and interior design by Jen Gunderson, fiveninetydesign.com
Cover image by Klara Maisch

Library of Congress Cataloging in Publication Data

Names: Goodfellow, Jessica, author.
Title: Whiteout / by Jessica Goodfellow.
Description: Fairbanks : University of Alaska Press, [2017] | Includes bibliographical references.
Identifiers: LCCN 2016056622 (print) | LCCN 2017002999 (ebook) | ISBN 9781602233270 (paper : alk. paper) | ISBN 9781602233287 (ebook)
Classification: LCC PS3607.O56345 A6 2017 (print) | LCC PS3607.O56345 (ebook) | DDC 811/.6dc23
LC record available at https://lccn.loc.gov/2016056622

for my mother, Judith Taylor Goodfellow
in memory of her brother
Stephen Arnold Taylor
August 12, 1944 – July 1967

TABLE OF CONTENTS

WHITEOUT

UNCANTICLE

Trees on the hillside, by the wind picked clean as fish bones—
Don't confuse, you said, *eliminate* with *illuminate*. But *look!*
at the fox, matted and dull as the downed leaves, not-quite-
vanishing behind a rock, to reappear *there, by the pine*, stitching
his way across the hillside, in and out of our sight line, our knowing.
He is not, this season, protected by summer's green blindfold
but exposed by winter's scant pastoral, its cold and barely
splintered light. *And look! now he's by that thicket*, but no,

again he's gone, and this time he stays gone, traceless. I wait,
and yes, like you, he stays gone. Did no one tell him a cubic mile
of fog is spun from less than a gallon of water? Did no one say, Do not
confuse *destruction* with *distraction*, *erasure* with *enrapture*?
For you, who said, *You are what you measure*, I measure this:
the way we record your death date as July 18 – July 28, 1967.

DISASTER

WHITE NOISE

Beneath the snowpack my uncle
rallies the other lost climbers
each tucked inside a felled icicle
like bullets riddling the landscape.

In Arizona, my uncle tells them,
power plants are named for cacti—
yucca and ocotillo,
the saguaro with a silhouette
sometimes mistaken for human.

The mountaineers nod in approval
which cracks them open about their faces.
They are surprised to find themselves
after all this time blinking.

Your families, my uncle says,
think of them busy making mobiles
from things they've melted
in their dishwashers.

Willing them warm, each man
tucked under his own blindfold
of snow, there are things
my uncle does not tell them:

that hot water is heavier than cold,
that the state flower of Alaska
is the alpine forget-me-not,
that earth is the only planet
not named for a god.

UNTRACEABLE

Either he burrowed under a skin of snow
that turned out to be the arch
of the foot of the storm.

Or the storm lulled, so he went for help,
stepping through the iced-over sky-
light of the underworld.

Or he was wind-snapped like a bedsheet
on a clothesline, then loosed, then tossed.
Later his sleeping bag was found wrapped

around a pole like a seahorse, tail-grasping at eel grass,
limbless against the current. *Tatsu no otoshigo*
that creature's called in Japanese—

child dropped by a dragon.

UNCLEAVED

Where a glacier has severed from itself is hard
to measure—no compass finds a crevasse, hid
beneath a snow bridge as thin as the eyelid of a god
forbid it blinks while my uncle's *on* it, then *in* it—
in the pupil of an eye ringed by a cold blue iris
of ice, and falling, falling, like a ruckus of light
through a silent chorus of stalactites—a fissure,
a seizure, an impasse he must not trespass—
he must not see from the inside this god's iris,
its concentric furrows, its collarette and crypts—
yes, the thin spots of the iris are called crypts—
let him not be encrypted deep in a deity's errant eye,
where we will never find him, never solve him
before a fresh eyelid of snow covers him
seamlessly, like the sheet hung over a mirror
in a house where someone's missing.

PHANTOM PANTOUM

The cover of *Time* magazine, front page of the *Denver Post*—
my uncle was suddenly everywhere, epic uncle of everyone,
of a nation eating their breakfast placidly, their own daring
nowhere to be found: not at Camp Seven, not on Denali Pass.

My uncle was suddenly everywhere, epic uncle of everyone,
while I was the niece of no body, because my uncle was also
nowhere to be found—not at Camp Seven, not on Denali Pass.
Also, he was everywhere, on *ABC News*, in the *Pittsburgh Gazette*,

while I was the niece of no body, because my uncle was also
not on McKinley's south summit, and not on Karstens Ridge.
Also, he was everywhere, on *ABC News*, in the *Pittsburgh Gazette*—
his nowhere was everywhere. My mother could not look.

Not on McKinley's south summit, and not on Karstens Ridge—
for days in the raging storm, rescuers could not look.
His nowhere was everywhere. My mother could not look.
What happened to those seven climbers? Their bodies were

for days in the raging storm. Rescuers could not look,
each wearing 45 miles of nerves in the snow, wondering,
what happened to those seven climbers? Their bodies were
swathed in the unknowable. Their everywhere was nowhere,

each 45 miles of nerves *where* in the snow? Wondering
became a sufferfest for the families—helpless, separated from,
swathed in the unknowable. Their everywhere was nowhere,
spent. By looking and not looking, absence became present,

became a sufferfest for the families, helpless, separated from
a nation eating their broken facts placidly, their own daring
spent by looking. And not looking, absence became present
on the cover of *Time* magazine, front page of the *Denver Post*.

THEORIES OF FLOW

The brain, Aristotle ruled,
was a system meant to cool
the heart. Hot heart.

Neuroscientists now name
the yawn a way to cool
the brain. Hot brain.

The words for *birth*
and *life* and *death*
end each in the rushing

sound of air pushed through
the mouth's constriction—
breath. Hot breath.

The word *breath* too
ends in that voiceless noise,
the unforgiving friction

fired between a body
and the air that it requires.
Body hot. Then not.

HOVER

Permutations of his death:
his body up, a human kite by the mountain's fist let go
his body down, an outlandish sand dollar, Vitruvian man under hoarfrost
his body, how many parts per million of the permafrost

At some point he must have known:
he'd never leave the mountain
he'd already left the mountain
he'd pierced the membrane between man and mountain

Whiteout, *noun:*

1. a blizzard, esp. in polar regions, that reduces visibilities to near zero
2. white correction fluid for covering typing or writing mistakes
3. a loss of color vision due to rapid acceleration, often before a loss of consciousness

Hover, canopy, the endless falling snow a shroud
What wish did the wind make
before tossing the coin of his body down
the well of forever?

SEARCH PARTY, CALLED OFF

In the either of ether or ice
he became not himself but his body.
He froze or he fell—in the never
of knowing, we pitch our tents.
We dwell in the hinge of weather
and whether. In each tent hangs
his photograph, its own kind of ice.
Beneath it we sleep, or try to

while he lies in the ever of winter
and vertigo. We dream the between
of his fingers twined on a breath-
emptied chest in the plain pine casket
we don't have—the only of winterkill.
We are winnowed—the wind
in widdershins spin; the clock hiding
its souvenirs in a blue wound.

UNCOLLECTED

They never found *his body*, we say, and NOT
they never found *him*. If seeing is believing, what's NOT

seeing? Some people, I've heard, at poetry readings
play a drinking game—taking a swig each time the word

body turns up in a poem. If they were reading this
they'd be drunk out of their minds by now—

that's how we say it: drunk out of their minds, NOT
drunk out of their bodies. Out of his mind with grief,

too, they said, when my grandfather almost stopped
speaking the year after the accident, staring into space

and saying nothing. No one could get drunk on that,
on the sober silence we cocoon around my uncle's absence.

Lost, like the Ten Tribes of Israel, like milk teeth—
ironically—as that's the one thing my grandfather has left

of his beloved son's body, of him: a small box of milk teeth,
each a tiny snow-slick mountain, faintly stained with blood.

HOW IT WOULD BE DIFFERENT IF WE HAD HIS BODY

Reading that the ancients knew the mountains
as *scars of the earth*,
we would not slowly nod.

This we would not imagine:
the mountain as magician,
my uncle and the others tucked
inside its snowy sleeve,
a row of stoic doves, waiting
for an incantation no one knows.

We could believe
again in the temporality
of winter.

Some of them, we were told,
must have settled their bodies
into snow caves
like clappers into bells they meant to ring
once the storm had cleared.
If we had his body, the chimes in
our minds would stop
their windy chaos.

We would not see one-way ladders
in our shadows,
leading down.

If we had his body,
what would be different
is nothing, *our* nothing.

Wakened by the wind,
we would not have
already been awake.

We could forget, for a moment,
that even the center of the eye—
the part that lets light in—
is a hole.

FARE

A coffin is an envelope
for sending off the body.
We do not have a body.

We have the skeleton of a balloon.
We have our breath, white on the window.
We cannot see through it.

In Japan, five- and fifty-yen coins
are hewn with holes in the center.
We can see through them.

These are the coins considered
lucky. Imagine that—a thing
missing its center is what's lucky.

I dreamed of a coffin filled
with five-yen coins,
so heavy we couldn't lift it.

When I woke, I took two five-yen coins
and sealed them in an envelope.
Absent of center, granting passage-

way to light, lucky—if that is
luck—these are the coins I would
place over his eyes, if we had a body.

THINGS THAT AREN'T SUPPOSED TO HAPPEN REMIND ME OF MY UNCLE

icicles from the eaves
drip a quiet canticle
chanting as they deliquesce
erasing themselves
alchemizing body
into sound

at night I wake,
                                        think I hear

MAP OF THE DISASTER SITE

I.
Here is Muldrow Glacier, and here
are Camps Six and Seven.

The dotted line running up this side
is the route of ascension.

Over there is Archdeacons Tower. Here
and here are probable sites of bivouac.

This is where his sleeping bag was sighted
but not recovered.

It was wrapped around a pole as though
a signal to no one.

X marks the axe—
also seen but not recovered,

like the bodies of three other climbers:
X X X — schemata of the mountain's stigmata.

II.
In theory, a map is useful: it renders two-
dimensional what exists in three dimensions,

or in this case, no dimensions, unless
we're counting time, which is like

wearing both shoes on one foot. In fact,
a map's convenient, able to be folded up

and carried in my pocket, opening and closing
like a lung. But in the end a map is useless,

only gravity's graffiti and snow's slow pentimento.
Unrepentant map, no X marks the mountain's fontanel,

its loosely woven selvage he fell through into the legend-
less depths of the wild mind, the memory   leaving us

only this permanent impermanence, this paper tattoo
breathing in and out the black ink of not knowing.

MORPHOLOGY

So many parts of the mountain
are named after the body—

the headwall, the lip, the flank,
the shoulder, and the brow.

The mountain even has a face,
where the face of our beloved

no more turns toward rumble
of far-off avalanche, nor tilts

in wonder at the alpenglow.
His furrowed brow's not found

atop a glacier, bent over a chessboard
on a day deemed unfit for travel.

Nor do his wide, pale eyes flinch
when one group heads for the summit,

the other leaves for lower camp,
while he alone attends the middle

on a day no one thought to deem
unfit for travel.

The mountain and our beloved
both had their north faces,

which might be why the storm could not
tell one from the other. Conjoined.

So many parts of the mountain
are named after the body.

This was not our only attempt
at incantation, about-face incarnation,

flesh made word.
We also say a river has a *mouth*

and a clock has *hands*—
potencies we ache to embody,

to cast in our own image
like gods.

MY MOTHER ADDS THE NAME OF HER BROTHER, MISSING ON DENALI SINCE 1967, TO HER PARENTS' HEADSTONE

(Recovered)
An abandoned mandolin leans against the wall, silent
as the shadow of a bell, bereft of the wayfaring fingers
that once mistook its highest note for north. On a sheer face,
recoverable: a sleeping bag, an ice axe, handholds of nothing.

(Unrecovered)
He who never thought to migrate, only wander,
is now not only citizen but mayor of the permafrost,
land where the only mail delivered must be written
on the inside of a snowflake.

(The name)
We have his name, which means *crown*. As in pinnacle
or peak of a mountain. As in the part of an anchor where
the arms join the shank, the lowest part. Our lowest part:
we have his name, but his body's anchored to the mountain.

(The date)
We have no date, and no creation myth. What we have
is this: a bird that does not catch fire on purpose,
the belief that each of us is born with a timetable
scrimshawed on the bones that cage the heart.

(The marker)
We could not bear his body down, its icy heights.
In lieu we craved a marker, a thing more still
than our sleepless minds, pitch-black pinwheels
blown through haphazardly by his windy ghost.

(The grave)
All calendars confuse time with space,
which is how they are rendered
finally useless, like a silver pendant bearing
(groundlessly) the Chinese character for empty.

(The body)
Grief's stark geometry: his frigid ribcage is the edge
between symmetric snowflakes and an asymmetric heart.
Still his long-absent torso hovers, beckoning, blocking
the door to winter, to forgetting.

TEN VARIATIONS ON A WEIGHT-BEARING AIR

VARIATION 1: WEIGHT BEARING AIR

What is a body anyway—
bacchanalia's abacus,
muscle circumspangled by nerves
that burn out, one by one,
like fireflies, like a string
of Christmas bulbs.

VARIATION 2: WEIGHT-BEARING AIR

Death, as predictable as wind—
afterward,
we drag around our phantom
limbs of grief, noctambulant,
and boot-eyed.

VARIATION 3: A WEIGHT BARING AIR

The first-ever headstones
had heft meant for holding
down the dead, as though
the living did not trust their own
memories.

VARIATION 4: A WAIT BEARING AIR

Good call, not trusting
your own memory,
the one that replaced a brother
with a blindfold,
sacrum with sacrament,
sinew with snow.

VARIATION 5: AWAIT BARING AIR

Whoever
translated *algebra*
not as
    a branch of mathematics in which arithmetical operations and
    relationships are generalized by using alphabetic symbols to represent
    unknown . . . members of specified sets . . .
                                        (unknown . . . members)
nor as
    the science of restoring what is missing and equating like with like
                                        (what is missing)
but as
    the reunion of broken parts—

whoever it was that made that facile choice
                                        (like with like)
find her
and break her.

VARIATION 6: A WEIGHT-BARING AIR

Body as angle of incidence,
as museum of echoes,
as stammer of tumblers
in an unlockable lock.
Body as creation myth of mirrors.

VARIATION 7: WEIGHT BARING AIR

Death, which had been effect,
now becomes cause.
An accidental pilgrim wanders
through the four seasons
as they
tessellate the decades.

VARIATION 8: WEIGHT BEARING HEIR

This is not an epicedium, sung only in the presence of the dead.
This is not an elegy, moving from grief toward relief.
This is not a threnody, which entails wailing.
This is not a monody, for one voice only.
This might be a lament, a spell for calling back the dead.
This could be a confession: if you hadn't had
a missing brother, I'd have
invented you
one.

VARIATION 9: A WEIGHT BEARING ERR

Body as rodeo of the soul,
as school for shadows,
as baptism by snow.
The body understands
it is dust
that teaches edges
to the wind.

VARIATION 10: A WEIGHT BARING ERR

A body flies
through the windshield of ice
that is tundra, time made space.
And disappears. In all directions
from the minute human-shaped hole,
the vast windshield splinters finely.
There is no seeing through it.

AFTERMATH

THE FOLD

In origami the mountain fold
folds down—constructing
an obstacle. The valley fold
folds up: receptacle.
The difference between
structure and stricture,
between paperweight
and wastepaper basket.

My family is silent
about our dead. Hardly
a word about an uncle,
a brother. We children were
to understand that meant:
he was beloved.
Silence as receptacle.

A paper creased
in mountain fold
can be turned upside down—
voilà! valley fold.
And all our dead tucked
safely inside. Save the one
whose body's lost
on the mountain,
the obstacle,
with which I have
confused the silence,
the absence.

Mountain, valley:
it is a matter
of which side you are on,
and if you have no body—
no matter—
you are on neither side.
You are the fold,
the stylus of silence
on which hinges both
our Cartesian cathedral
and the vertex of our vortex.

Chasm and scaffold,
cornice and crevasse,
the steep pitch of life
and its inverse, its obverse.
Observe, mortals:
the edge. Welcome
to our fold.

EVER AFTERMATH

The math of aftermath is subtraction—
disaster, catastrophe, ruin:
loss, loss, and loss.

It wasn't always so.
Math came from the Old English
for *mowing*—when aftermath was a second crop

in the same season on the same land
as the first brutal harvest. Then,
the math of aftermath was addition.

It was called also *rowen*, *rowett*,
and *lattermath*, and when left to lie too long
on the ground, it was known as *fog*.

Fog—a word, perhaps, for *our* aftermath—
his body left to lie forever in ice
on Denali's one-way ladder.

And we, who grew up after his harvesting,
his subtractive aftermath,
his fog, we who grew up

in our family's silent grief,
were added to the scene like sheep
set to graze in the foreground of Stonehenge.

HEAD COUNT

My six sisters, my brother, and I used to joke
our mother couldn't count higher than eight—
her frantic number-line looping, a litany—
we laughed at what we did not know
                                        was grief.

In the way Wile E. Coyote never falls
until he looks down, and sees the cliffless nothing—
our mother had looked and we hadn't.

        Counting seven white horses, she said,
unlocked a wish, and I wondered if her seventh horse
carried in her eighth child, like each of the others,
an insufficient stand-in.

        Horses as white as ghosts—a hint,
        like the pet rabbits and the goldfish,
        so we could learn, she said, responsibility,
        which means both dependability
        and blame.

                Monsters under the bed? She said, yes.
        Helium balloons with the hardware store's logo
gone forever into the blue? Also, yes. You let go, didn't you?

        And here's how she taught us
to play hide-and-seek: another, she said,
had gone ahead and was playing
hide-and-hide;
                we would just seek-and-seek.

UNCONSOLED

In my dreams my uncle rides
the glacier like a surfboard,
arms wide-open like a savior.

If he had lived, he might have
solved my childhood. He dismounts
the mountain, astonished to see me

no longer two years old and mittened,
hands hampered by love. I'm sorry, I say.
We almost never speak of you.

It's okay, he says. A snowman is a man
built of snow. A snow angel is made
by taking snow away.

UNCALCULABLE

Rock. Paper. Scissors.
Mountain. Snow. Death.

Snow beats mountain
by shrouding it in white.

Death beats snow
by taking away its prisoners.

Mountain beats death,
outlasting it and its memory.

Nothing beats everything.
Around and around it goes—

a braid of bad reckoning,
a lasso of logic, a noose.

This poem I wrote on paper.
Paper beats memory beats death

but only until paper crumbles
or memory's vessel collapses.

In the meantime, paper can be
creased into a blindfold, but why

bother, when the deciding round is played
against the already invisible fist of god.

TEST

Mrs. Yeager's handout of college prep vocab words
was meant as an *onerous* task for a *neophyte*, a *germane lexicon*,
but I *ascertained* first what had been my uncle's initials: S A T.·
I heard no more of the lecture, repeated silently his *moniker*.
Was this (a) *auspicious*; (b) *ominous*; (c) merely *benign*?

My mother's only story: how my uncle, between all-
night shifts at the post office and *arduous* college courses,
used to rouse and feed an infant me, his hand to my mouth.
Otherwise she kept a silence in which I learned *ambiguous*,
lugubrious, and *truncate*. Through my uncle's absence
I memorized *doleful*, *evanescent*, and *curtailed* by heart.

"Choose the best answer from the following." The sentence suggests
there *is* a best answer for an empty mouth. Mortality is
(a) *conditional*; (b) *congenital*; (c) *incompatible*; (d) *superfluous*.
Death is (a) *insatiable*; (b) *inexorable*; (c) *ineffable*; (d) *immutable*.
I am (a) the niece of no body; (b) death's little *dilettante*;
(c) *consanguine* with hoarfrost; (d) kin to white noise.

MOST DAYS

Most days even the locals can't find Denali on the horizon,

shrouded as it is by a layer of fog, a hazy white
(like the tissue-paper protector atop his diploma,
granted after the fact, like a death certificate).

Most days no one sights the mountain

wearing a curtain of clouds
(like a veil for a bride he left us to elope with).

The mountain is almost always

swaddled day after day in clouds
(like an infant cocooned in flannel—
my uncle's firstborn, brought forth in sorrow).

Most days even the locals can't find Denali on the horizon,

can't find the place where his body can't be found.

Most days I don't think of Denali at all,

don't remember him, twenty-two years old forever
(younger than I am now, a skinny hitchhiker
with a handmade sign: GOING TO SEE NEW NIECE).

That new niece was my sister, not me.

I'm the one wondering, Tissue paper?
What kind of protection is that?
(Most days I don't think of him at all: it's that kind.)

QUAKING ASPEN

FOR MY GRANDMOTHER

Rarely survives at elevations of less than 1500 feet. Found, in the US, at 5000–12,000 feet
my mother's antique-green piano my daily hour of Bartok, Mozart
under an oil painting of a quaking aspen grove trees caught
mid-tremble my great-grandmother as the painter—
even then my family
had a penchant for altitude, for height
How beautiful upon the mountains

Its smooth white bark marked by thick black scars, where low branches have pruned themselves
among her losses three children each before the age of three
in the flood, her husband rescued the family but could not save
himself the year post-flood
she and her daughter, ten years old—my grandmother— the hospital
nothing
to do but think of the flood the lowlands
no wonder she preferred high places
the trembling
How beautiful upon the mountains are the feet of him

Leaves nearly heart-shaped, with edges finely saw-toothed
never to remarry despite a wealthy suitor
her family confounded by her devotion to
the gone and ungospelled husband owner of a livery
just as factories rolled out
the nation's first affordable cars
thy watchmen shall lift up the voice

Leaves with flattened petioles, even in the most gentle breeze appearing to tremble
struggling three remaining children a schoolteacher's salary
little cash for turpentine and canvas
for viridian green titanium white still she found a way
to paint the quaking aspens
to make the trembling visible
they shall see eye to eye

A stand of aspens = one single organism, stretching up to twenty acres, roots entangled under-ground
my grandmother, her daughter lost a father three siblings
and then her only son turned his eyes cerulean
like his grandmother's
to the mountains raw umber
turned the body she had given him, trembling
to the high places to his entangled roots
made bare his holy arm

All aspens of one root system have the same branching structure; in autumn, all changing to the exact same color at the exact same time
what color, loss— white marked by thick black scars
or white a blank canvas of snow marred by an orange sleeping bag
by an ice axe scattershot
like scars upon the icy landscape pruning itself
ye waste places of Jerusalem

A stand of aspens can live to be thousands of years old—might be the oldest known living thing
aspens caught mid-quake in an antique-green frame antique-green piano
how beautiful Bartok, Mozart
to dream of feet upon the mountains of him
his feet upon the mountains
yellow ochre
oldest living things, trembling roots entwined
my inky scrawl like black scars on a white page
my great-grandmother's black paint on white canvas
the aspens quaking
at the exact same time
all the ends of the earth

THINGS THAT AREN'T SUPPOSED TO HAPPEN REMIND ME OF MY UNCLE

early December
an orange globe dangles
from a garden tree,
not an ornament but
a persimmon,
out of season,

dusted with snow

LIKE ANY HISTORY, A FAMILY HISTORY REPEATS

For example, my uncle's ten-day disappearance
before being given up for dead turned out to be
good practice for when my brother, his namesake,
for a fortnight vanished.

There were differences, of course—
my brother turned himself in,
while my mother's brother was seen again never.
His was an act of God, my brother's an act of will.
Also, no one dared look for my uncle
sealed behind Denali's raging mask,
while everyone searched for my brother—
friends, family, and police with their forty-eight-state APB.

The Ten'a tribe also speaks of a boy on the run,
fleeing not in stolen cars, but by canoe.
Their young man too was pursued, not by the law
but by an envious warlord and his magic spear.
Lacking shield, the boy conjured a vast ocean wave
that became a great wall of stone: Denali.

There it is: the third vertex of the triangle,
from uncle to brother to myth, and back to uncle:
the trope of the young man on a journey,
a braid of history, history, and myth.

Here is a brief history of mirrors:
an early man with an ache to see his own face
gazed at water pooled in a bowl painted black,
or looked hard at highly polished obsidian.
For what we cannot bear to look at directly,
myth is history's first ancient mirror,
reflection of the same unfleeable triangle,
sum of three interlocked vertices:
the self, the dark, the familiar.

FIVE WAYS OF RESISTING NOTHING

To photograph is to write with light: *the moon tattooed on a slick membrane*
inconstancy bested by incandescence

To remember is to write with windows: *stain of invisible pixels*
lashed to a vanished direction

To regret is to write with white noise: *swathe of tundra's sterile gauze*
masking the heart's useless mantra

To forget is to write with snow: *a crystalline blister of oblivion*
sealing a haphazard landscape

To dream is to write with revolving doors: *a shuffling of alphabets and archetypes*
in the Möbius strip of the mind

Against the five ways of resisting nothing: *nothing resists in return*
there is no suffering like this

THE BEGINNER'S GUIDE TO ENDINGS

My grandparents drove for a day and a half
to view the life-sized cardboard cutout
of my teenaged grandfather, his paper arm
about the cinched waist of the two-dimensional
Edith Egan, winners in the Lindy hop contest
on the world's largest dance floor at Saltair.

I was there that night too, my grandmother said.
With. A. Date. Also, *That appliqued waistband*
flattered Edith; she was never quite that slim.
My grandfather only looked at the young [im]poster
of himself, smiled, then got in his car and drove
the day and a half it took to get back home.

Spinoza said, *The chief endeavor of the mind*
is . . . to affirm the existence of the body.
The eight thousand terra-cotta warriors buried
with the first emperor of China each bore
a different face. John Ciardi said, *I realized*
the photographer is photographing himself.

Why did I use time instead of distance to measure
my grandparents' journey? Why *a day and a half* rather
than *seven hundred miles*? My grandfather once told me
if a body falls for twenty stories, when it hits the earth
it sounds the same as a door dropped from that height.
Of all the things he might have said, he said *a door*.

MEANWHILE

Here is a photo of my second son.
He has the same angled ears

as my uncle.
No one has ever said so.

Cousins, aunts, all look at him long and hard
and then don't say so.

My sister cuts tiny fabric squares,
sews them back together in a quilt.

Her son, younger than mine,
thinks this is crazy. He points

to a blue square, says
my soccer shirt from last year.

He smiles as he points,
looking just like his father—

everybody says so. My son wonders
why I don't quilt, don't slice

and rearrange ordinary days
we won't recall into mosaics

that we will. The opposite
of remember, I once read,

is dismember. I am silenced
by the unspoken family pledge:

until we have a body
we cannot say *uncle.*

Meanwhile, my son picks at his ear,
thinks he looks like no one.

K STREET HANGOUT

FOR MY GRANDFATHER

No magpie hankers for this life,
rough weave of paycheck and prayer book.

You say there were fireflies in trees,
a hapless uncle's engineless car

and a steep hill to roll it down.
Come dusk the kids one by one peeled off

leaving only the gypsies of Sisyphus,
pushing that runaway wreck up the avenues,

last chase of axle and chassis, for one more joyride.
You thought gravity was your friend. You thought

your mother's voice would always call you
home. You believed you could choose

your own burden, could escape the double-helix hex.
When your son chose his own burden to carry

up a mountain, you thought you could always call him
home. Instead, all that returned to you was

your sturdy engineless grief. Absence, you understand now,
is not a hole, but a weight. All day you heave it

toward nightfall, toward sleep. Come morning,
there it is again, undiminished, fallen back of its own weight.

WHAT MY GRANDFATHER HEARD

O THE MIND, MIND HAS MOUNTAINS
–GERARD MANLEY HOPKINS

My grandfather heard
from his married daughter
who'd heard from an old family friend
who'd heard on the radio that
his own only son was counted among
the missing on Mount McKinley.
It was the first intimation of trouble.

Except that
a few nights before
my grandfather woke
in the Chicago dark
to the voice of his son
calling, *Father, Father, help.*
His son was, he knew, in Alaska,
yet he heard his voice as clearly
as fear. My grandfather woke
his wife to say, "Our boy, he is in trouble."

Born in the first generation
to believe in angels
and airplanes equally,
my grandfather knew breath
hanging white in cold air
could cast shadows on the ground.
What he didn't expect
was the absence of breath
to stain the days with umbra.

My grandfather would go on
to lose also his hearing, as if
his ears couldn't bear
one more futile request.
Instead, they subtracted the sounds
of the world one by one,
and let rise, instead,
a susurrus in his mind,
echoes of an Arctic wind
blowing always in him.

22

What we do not know about a missing loved one becomes all that we know.
– T. S. Eliot

1. The number 22 has a pleasing symmetry and logic: two of the number 2, in a row. This is called *translation symmetry*, the repeating of patterns, which is different from *reflection, or mirror, symmetry*. Other numbers have translation symmetry, like 11 and 33, but 11 is not one 1, and 33 is not three 3s. 333 has both translation symmetry and a numerical logic like 22 but, adding now a third criteria, most people do not live to be 333 years old.

2. My mother was 1 of 2 siblings. Her younger brother, my uncle, was born the year my mother turned 4 years old, in 1944. 44 = 22 × 2.

3. An embryonic human heart starts to beat on the 22nd day. Thus my uncle's heart most likely began beating when he was 22 days in the womb. My uncle's heart stopped beating when he was 22 years in the world, which is also sort of symmetric, but not at all pleasing, and not at all logical.

4. My uncle was a sickly child, but with the help of his family and his doctor, Herman I. Laff, he reached young adulthood, though it had been thought improbable. This was achieved by periodically draining my uncle's lungs throughout his childhood. Contrary to what you might expect, lungs do not exhibit reflection symmetry. In fact, the right lung has 3 lobes but the left only 2. This is to leave room for the heart.

5. As an adult, my uncle was tall and thin, with prominent ears on a face longer and more narrow than average. The average circumference of the human head is 22 inches. The human head does not generally exhibit perfect reflection symmetry, though the most beautiful human faces, as judged by other humans, are as symmetrical as possible. What *does* exhibit perfect reflection symmetry in all directions is a circle.

6. The circumference of a circle divided by its diameter is a fixed ratio called π. This is commonly approximated by the fraction 22/7. When π is represented as a decimal, it has no end, and no repeating patterns in its infinite string of digits. That is, there is no translation symmetry. A number like this we call *irrational*. 22/7 reminds me that a human head, a human mind, splintered in 7 directions, might also be called *irrational*.

7. When I think about the number 22, the age at which my mother's only sibling died, my mind is splintered in 7 directions, 1 each for *my* siblings, and there is no end to my thinking, though I admit to some repetition.

8. I think about my grandfather, my uncle's father, who died when he was (22 × 4) years old. I think of Jesus Christ, who died when he was (22 × $^3/_2$) years old.

9. Jesus grew up in a Jewish household, and mostly likely was literate in Hebrew. While there are those who insist on an Aramaic-only Jesus, others contend that while reading and discussing the Torah with the elders at the temple, Jesus must have been using Hebrew. There are, in the Hebrew alphabet, 22 letters.

10. Jesus died by crucifixion, on order of Pontius Pilate, the Roman emperor. The Roman numeral for 22 is XXII. This does not have reflection symmetry, though it establishes an easily recognizable pattern. My uncle was a believer in Jesus, as were his parents, and their parents, and so on. This also establishes an easily recognizable pattern.

11. You may be thinking, "Just because you see the number 22 everywhere doesn't mean it has significance." Yes, but only because the number 22 already had significance to me did I start seeing it everywhere. This is almost a classic catch-22 situation.

12. The term *catch-22* was coined in Joseph Heller's 1961 satirical novel *Catch-22*, set during World War II. World War II is often abbreviated as WWII. If you replace the W's with X's, you get XXII, which should be by now a familiar pattern.

13. During the period from 1953 to 1961 when Joseph Heller was writing *Catch-22*, his contemporary, Kurt Vonnegut Jr., published *The Sirens of Titan*, a novel about the richest man alive in 22nd-century America. Titan is the largest moon of Saturn and was named for the Titans of Greek mythology. Something else named for the Greek Titans is the chemical element Titanium, which has as its symbol Ti and as its atomic number 22.

14. While my uncle majored in physics in college, he must also have known the rudiments of chemistry. He must have known that in the periodic table, Titanium lies between Scandium and Vanadium. He might have known, or at least have guessed, that Scandium was named after Scandinavia. As a mountain climber, he might also have known that the mountains in Scandinavia are largely alpine tundra, also found in Denali National Park, home to Mount McKinley, which is where my uncle died.

15. My uncle also must have known that the symbol for Vanadium is V, the 22nd letter of the alphabet. The letter *V* occurs twice in the words *vive*, *viva*, and *vivat*, which come from the Romance languages, and occur in phrases as such "*viva X*," meaning "long live *X*." My uncle did not live long. No rescue party came. Instead his body lies frozen now in ice, unrecovered.

16. Things which lay frozen in ice for 100 years, but which were finally recovered, include the 22 unprocessed photographic negatives of Sir Shackleton's lost Ross Sea party. This party was abandoned in the Antarctic from 1914 to 1917, when its ship blew out to sea during a blizzard. If you want to see these 22 recovered photographs, which were freed from a solid block of ice, restored, and developed in 2013, here is the URL: http://www.nzaht.org/AHT/ross-sea-party-lost-photos/.

17. A URL, or uniform resource locator, is a way of specifying addresses on the worldwide web. URLs have their own coding using the ASCII character set. The URL code %22 specifies the quotation mark. I cannot quote anything my uncle ever said. I cannot remember hearing him speak, even though for a summer during his college years he lived with my parents, my older sister, and me, and though he came home from his job sorting mail on the night shift at the post office and fed me my bottle.

18. Because my grandmother grieved for him so deeply, we almost never spoke of my uncle. I do not know very much about him. But my mother did once tell me that his favorite board game was Monopoly. Monopoly was modeled after Atlantic City, New Jersey, and is composed of hotels and houses lying on 22 different streets.

19. You perhaps think now, with my mention of Monopoly, that I've verged on the ridiculous. It is true that I see the number 22 *everywhere*; it's my way of seeing my uncle everywhere. This is how it is with secondhand sorrow. Firsthand sorrow has a focus, a place to be placed, but secondhand sorrow, especially when never spoken of, is more diffuse, less understood, and thus more likely to be placed onto things to which it has no connection.

20. Should I try *not* to see connections where they don't exist? Should I strive *not* to infuse numbers with meaning? I am not the first to do this: numerologists tend to classify as 22 a person who feels that she lives in 2 different worlds, 1 mundane and 1 fantastical. Tarot card readers, with their 22 major arcana cards, sometimes interpret the 22nd card as *The Fool* and sometimes as *The World*.

21. In another system of making sense of the world, the 22nd Psalm is called A Cry of Anguish and a Song of Praise. Jesus, when dying, quoted from the 1st verse of the 22nd Psalm: "My God, my God, why have You forsaken me?"

22. So we have reached the 22nd item on this list. It will be the last item, and also it will end abruptly. It will exhibit a pattern, but not mirror symmetry, so as to leave room for the heart.

GLACIAL ERASURE

To make the suffering visible.
– Jean Valentine

NOCTURNE WITH INERTIA

Birches reflect on the lake
like ragged strips of silver
peeling from the back of a mirror.

The long jaw of a wolf
lies in the snow, picked clean
by vestigial scavengers. *Winter*

is by far the oldest of the seasons—
monkish and rawboned, counting
backward to: rend, render, surrender.

THE RELIEF MAP FAILS TO RELIEVE

All maps view their subjects from above,
while a glacier glissandos always downward—
gouging as it goes, unzipping the underworld.

The void's already hoisted its *No Vacancy* sign.
All those still corseted by torsos cannot cross,
cannot join the vacated in their icy cradles.

The relief map flattens the landscape on the page,
contour lines erasing one dimension, then
another: time. Each charted mountain peak

radiates a dense concentric whorl. Like a pebble
dropped into a bottomless lake. Tree rings.
Fingerprints. What's left after tree or thief is gone.

UNCHRONICLED

The human species, in total, climbed out of the landscape
and into the portrait. Each human, in particular, falls
out of a portrait to return to the landscape—
a counterclockwise canticle of particles.

My uncle, for example, climbed the one-way ladder
DENALI. And vanished. The well-behaved dead
are supposed to lie below us, not above,
so we do not like to speak of it. DENIAL.

We do not like to speak of not speaking of it.
We put ellipses in place of what is missing,
then want to hide the ellipses, but with what?
For a long time there was no headstone.

The well-behaved dead are supposed to leave us
a body. When they don't, we do not like
to speak of it. Pallbearers stand in an uncertain circle,
staring at a shadow, a pall, cast by no body.

We cannot hoist a shadow on our shoulders.
We cannot pale this pall. We do not like to
speak of it, of what the body bodes: of what
no body bodes, the canting of portrait into landscape.

HERESY

The prevalent model has the soul as nougat
and around it, like chocolate, the body wrapped. Rapt.
Intuitive—the body's visible while the soul is not.

But imagine, instead, the body as speaker,
the soul as a kind of velvet surround sound.
Think: body equals nucleus; soul, electron cloud.

You protest—this theory suggests the body
preexists the soul. Yes: suppose you only
get a soul once you need one.

Imagine the body as irritant, a grain of sand inside
an oyster that conjures in response a cosmic pearl.
Let the soul be glow-in-the-dark dark.

You who hate this proposal must never
have lost somebody whose body was never
recovered. You want the body as cage

that releases, finally, the soul. You want
the soul as body, the body as tattoo.
Your body is soul's amulet, while mine

is vice versa. You see the soul as map
of the body's limited terrain; I see the body
as map of the measureless parish of soul,

body as an anchor in the sea. The body
can perish; the soul cannot. *Aha!* you say,
here we agree. But in your version,

the body says to the soul, *I will not let you go*
unless you bless me, while I struggle to learn,
like Zeno of Elea, not to distinguish between

a body and the space in which it is.

MADONNA AND PARTICLE CHILD : MY GRANDFATHER OUTLIVES HIS SON

Substance *is that which cannot be predicated of anything or be said to be in anything :*
Fried Egg on the Plate without the Plate.

Quantity *is the extension of an object, and may be either discrete or continuous :*
Self-Portrait Being Duplicated into Three.

Quality *is the determination that characterizes the nature of an object :*
All Shapes Derive from the Square.

Relation *is the way one object may be related to another :*
Hairdresser Depressed by the Persistent Good Weather.

Place *is position in relation to the surrounding environment :*
Cathedral of Thumbs.

Time *is position in relation to the course of events :*
The Triangular Hour.

Position *is a condition of rest resulting from an action. Thus position may be taken as the end point for the corresponding action :*
Face of Mae West Which May Be Used as an Apartment.

State *means a condition of rest resulting from an affection. The term is, however, frequently taken to mean the determination arising from the physical accoutrements of an object: one's shoes, one's arms, etc. Traditionally, this category is also called a habitus (from Latin* habere, *to have) :*
The Chromosome of a Highly Colored Fish's Eye Starting the Harmonious Disintegration of the Persistence of Memory.

Action *is a production of change in some other object (or in the agent itself* qua *other) :*
The Pharmacist of Ampurdan in Search of Absolutely Nothing.

Affection *is the reception of change from some other object. Aristotle's examples make clear that action is to affection as the active voice is to the passive voice—as* acting is to being acted on :
Polyhedron. Basketball Players Being Transformed into Angels (Assembling a Hologram—the Central Element).

UNCERTAINTY PRINCIPLE

ON THE CHANGE OF THE MOUNTAIN'S OFFICIAL NAME
FROM MOUNT MCKINLEY TO DENALI

There is always a tradeoff. In physics, for example,
the more precisely known a particle's momentum,
the fuzzier its location. The Malagasy must have traded

in something bitter to name their consecrated tree
kakazotsi fantata—tree whose name nobody knows.
What *we* don't know is where our beloved lies

atop a mountain, though we know his momentum:
zero. We've had to learn a new name, this week,
for his unknown resting spot, and the new name is *Denali.*

A better moniker than *McKinley*, though better still might
have been *mountain whose name nobody knows.*
Denali comes from a Kuyukon word meaning "to be

tall"—it's a *verb.* A verb by definition has momentum while
a mountain *is* location. Still, we fail to sieve truth from grief,
having only traded one cold shroud for another.

FACTS ABOUT ALASKA

Alaska: Continuous Entity

Alaska is Aleut for "shores where the sea breaks its back." Ocean's a perpetual motion machine where it wrestles land. Elsewhere a blue raft, bereft, it drifts through warp and weft of briny latitudes and longitudes, longing. If the opposite of a keyhole is a gangplank. If between *alive* and *dead* there is nothing more than *presumed dead* and *missing*.

Alaska: Binary Pair

Alaskan bears are said to be left-handed. Its sundogs come in pairs, equidistant illusions, like *alive* and *dead*. The northern lights are charged particles pinging the atmosphere, careless of towns below with twenty-four hours of daylight and towns with twenty-four hours of dark. If the opposite of a silhouette is a blindfold. Alaska's motto—*North to the Future*—does not say what lies south, where the past went, or if the people left there can be found.

Alaska: Liminal Space

Among the cheatgrass and the bittercress, the gray wolf holds its breath, an empty turnstile in an empty field. If the opposite of a spiral is another spiral. Forget *alive* and *dead*. Follow folklore: trace in space a spiral to catch a dragonfly, Alaska's state insect. But what can you draw to bring back the *presumed dead*, the *missing*? With hinges and doors, masks of the Haida tribe hid sometimes faces within other faces, human inside wolf, or raven. Behind that, the bearer of the mask, twice hidden: behind a bandage of snow, of years.

UNREACHABLE

REGRET HAS TO BE USELESS
OR IT'S NOT REALLY REGRET.
– SIMONE DE BEAUVOIR

Rescuers did not find my uncle's body.
But they found his axe at an icy altitude
impossible to navigate without one.

A little higher up, they found my uncle
's sleeping bag at an altitude
unsurvivable without one.

You likely have a pen in purse or pocket.
Take it out and write a list of all
you need at your present altitude.

Next, change altitudes. Now, make another list:
the two biggest regrets of your life.
Take your time. Get it right. Because

here is all you need to know about need:
That list of regrets—cross one off.
You are going to need that space later.

NOCTURNE WITHOUT COUNTEREXAMPLE

The mechanical oracle of moon
spools its rumors of change
that is not
ruinous.

The chronically unchronicled
wait patiently
as smog rusts the stars
that staple up the night.

Each heart beats:
bamboo /
bamboo—
sealing one emptiness
after another
into manageable chambers.

GLACIAL ERASURE

As he climbed up, the glacier
under his feet was inching down.
If he'd kept moving, he could have
scaled that ice escalator
and never noticed.
He did not keep moving.

1967. Experts estimated
the glacier would one day drift,
with its accidental stowaways,
to the lowlands—
like Dali's molten clock sliding
over a draped figure, a body recumbent,
in *The Persistence of Memory*.

Instead, melting glaciers empty
out their pockets, littering the landscape
with detritus and dead relatives.
The glacier that erased my uncle
soon will be erased, unfolded—
vacant of weather and weight,
roof become floor become flora
of a habitat as fluid
as memory.

TALKEETNA

East of the railroad, across from the airstrip,
a whitewashed telephone pole's been planted
in the cemetery. Unconnected. Dialing no one.

Carved by chainsaw, two wooden figures
scale the pole, wearing cedar crampons,
wielding wooden rope and axe.

This is the town that says the last good-bye
to mountaineers headed for Denali.
Climb high, sleep low is the unofficial motto:
the wooden figures embody one end of that spectrum.
The graves below disembody the other. Over there

is the weatherproofed memorial board, listing year
by year, name by name, the mountain's
quarry, its claim. Thirty-five percent
are bodies unrecovered. They will never
again sleep low.

This town that didn't have a bathtub until 1923
has at a local inn a Dead Man's Wall, complete
with photos. Or, more correctly, incomplete—
with photos.

Back at the cemetery, a carved raven tops the pole—
the only creature other than human seen
at the mountain's highest points, a bird cunning enough
to dig up buried caches meant for later.
This is a last reminder of what any climber could
meet at any time—a thief.

NOCTURNE WITHOUT U-TURN

one bouquet of vacancy, one lungful
of fleeting—the trees go up
in flaming foliage, then are barren,
burnt as only the cold can burn

one tightrope of solstice, one caveful
of vespers—the aspens
with their ten thousand wrought mouths
are organ pipes exhaling white noise

one siphoning of light, one cusp
of dusk's null hypothesis, each being
returns home under a moon
of lone imagining

A BRIEF HISTORY OF RISK

The Japanese say it is
a giant thrashing catfish
that stirs up earthquakes.

Hazard is from the Arabic
for *dice*, thrown down
in a tiny earthquake, a thrashing.

Less clear is the origin of *risk*—
perhaps from the Greek for *soldier's*
fortune, following the Arabic

of *that which God allots*,
stemming from Middle Persian
for *daily bread*. Or maybe *risk*

is from Italian via Latin for *cliff*,
or from Greek for *perils to avoid*
at sea, such as a giant catfish.

Centuries of uncertainty were up-
ended suddenly, and *fate* rechristened
as *probability*, when Fermat and Pascal

reckoned the Problem of Points: how to
split the ante of a game of chance,
like every game of chance—

> *Give us this day our daily risk*
> *and forgive us our shivers*
> *as we foreclose our futures*—

interrupted.

PHOTOS OF MEN BEFORE DISASTERS

1. The Ross Sea Party, 1913–17

From hundred-year-old ice a negative is peeled
then glazed with silver gelatin to unghost a bearded face.
Black mold licks the edges of a ragged snowscape—
Hut Point Peninsula, rogue ship *Aurora* in the foreground,
the bearded geologist leaning on its rails,
squinting at the camera, or past it. This is before
everything went wrong. The geologist's shoulders hunch
against the cold or the unknowing. A black smear
blurs sky, ice, and sea with vessel. To its far left
one arm and a shoulder of a shipmate, but no head.

2. The Wilcox Expedition, 1967

All twelve climbers are in this picture captured—
my uncle on the farthest left, wearing a red cap
shaped roughly like Denali, looming in the background.
His shoulders hunch but he is smiling,
squinting at the camera, or past it. This is before
everything went wrong—before the storm:
no one yet knowing which men would harbor
in the throat of god, wondering if he'd swallow,
and which would be across the hostile glacier sewn
like seeds in ice, sealed: separate, and rootless.

3. SS *Andrea Doria*, 1956

Here he is in cowboy hat and faux leather chaps,
a four-year-old Hopalong Cassidy. In this one, he's survived
jumping from a ceiling joist, arm pressed in plaster cast.
And this is the night he never slept, but hunched
around the radio as the *Andrea Doria* sank, ear turned
toward the speaker, eyes set gravely at the camera, or past it.
Here his mortarboard sails high above his parents' heads,
only two months before—but every photo here is him before
the disaster. We must not think this way. We must not notice
how in every photograph, the camera looks at us, and just past us.

NINE VIEWS OF DENALI

THE MOUNTAINS ARE ALIVE.
– CLAY DILLARD, PILOT AT
TALKEETNA AIR TAXI

1.
The mountain appears
through a venetian blind
of clouds—stripes of weather,
granite, snow.

2.
Mountain and sky the same
indigoes and whites
as the Blue Marble.
Fast-moving clouds are too high
to hide the peaks, but their shadows
sweep across the ridges—
the opposite of spotlights.

3.
Thick clouds hide all
but shifting glimpses
of the mountain, mottled white
and gray as the fifteen stones
at Ryoanji's Zen garden,
which from no angle
can all be seen at once.

4.
The clear blue slate of Wonder Lake
twins the sky. Counting
the reflection there are two
Denalis. My uncle could be
anywhere.

5.
Fish-scale moon
above Denali at midnight—
iridescent, incandescent,
partly darkled—
a frozen fire
and the spark that has escaped it.

6.
Wind shuffles the clouds
in a cosmic shell game
while we wager:
under which thunderhead
does the summit lie.

7.
The mountain's north faces
have ridges crisp as datelines—
ash blue todays on one side,
white nothings on the other.

8.
The blank white pages of Denali,
Foraker, and Hunter are smudged
across their bottom margins
by the inky scrawl of smaller ridges—
scribbles of unreadable runes.

9.
Behind us, the park road
winds toward the mountain
like a fuse.

AMERICAN DUSK

Beneath a stagger of stars the herd untangles,
hooves throbbing the prairie's dull drumhead,
grave as the heart's marginalia. The day unhitches
from reason. Pivot and swivel of senses
are over. Darkness laps at the edges.

The glass beads of heaven's black abacus
slide slowly toward rote constellations. Turning back
toward the lit house, where linen solves nothing,
recall that while *matter tells space how to curve,*
and *space teaches matter to move*, the word *endless*

isn't.

ACKNOWLEDGMENTS

Sincere thanks to the editors of the following journals in which poems have appeared (sometimes in earlier forms and/or with different titles):

The Adroit Journal: "Map of the Disaster Site"
Arsenic Lobster: "The Beginner's Guide to Endings," "K Street Hangout"
The Baltimore Review: "Nocturne without Counterexample"
B O D Y: "Uncollected" (under the title "Not Seeing")
Columbia College Literary Review: "Uncalculable," "Unchronicled"
DMQ Review: "A Brief History of Risk," "Uncleaved" (under the title "Crevasse"), "Untraceable" (under the title "Three Blizzard Scenarios")
Echolocation: "22"
Hartskill Review: "Photos of Men Before Disasters," "White Noise"
Hunger Mountain – VCFA Journal of the Arts: "The Fold," "Theories of Flow"
Memorious: "Fare"
Nashville Review: "Unreachable" (under the title "Altitude")
Naugatuck River Review: "Head Count"
New Madrid: "Ever Aftermath," "Morphology," "Nocturne with Inertia"
One: "Nocturne without U-Turn"
Pool Poetry: "American Dusk," "Heresy," "Quaking Aspen," "Ten Variations on a Weight-Bearing Air"
The Quarterday Review: "Phantom Pantoum"
Queen's Mob Tea House: "Madonna and Particle Child : My Grandfather Outlives His Son"
Rappahannock Review: "Meanwhile"
Rattle: *Poetry for the 21st Century*: "Unconsoled" (under the title "Wakening")
The Southern Review: "Most Days," "Test," "What My Grandfather Heard"
Thrush Poetry Journal: "Hover," "My Mother Adds the Name of Her Brother, Missing on Denali since 1967, to Her Parents' Headstone," "Uncanticle" (under the title "Pairs")
Tinderbox Poetry Journal: "How It Would Be Different If We Had His Body"
Tishman Review: "Facts about Alaska," "Glacial Erasure"
Valparaiso Poetry Review: "The Relief Map Fails to Relieve," "Search Party, Called Off"

"Nine Views of Denali" was written during a writer's residency at Denali National Park and Preserve and has appeared in promotional materials for the Park Service.

All my thanks goes to Kelly Cressio-Moeller, Shane McRae, Lisa Fay Coutley, Peter and Heather Mallet, MaryKatherine Callaway, and Ava L. Haymon, for writing advice; the staff of Denali National Park and Preserve, in particular to Jay Elhard, Cinnamon Dockham, Frank Soos, and Don Striker, for kindness and generous hospitality; Jennifer Bradley, Iris Neary, and Simon and Jenna Hamm for authenticity, for keeping it real; Amy Simpson, Peggy Shumaker, Laura Walker, and Krista West for believing in my work; Joeth Zucco for copy editing contributions; Perry and Beth Taylor, James and Judith Goodfellow, Jamie Rippy, Tracy Slater, and Cameron Morse for unending support. And, as always, all the love and gratitude in my heart go to the very patient Naohiko, Taiyo, and Hiyugo Ueno.

NOTES

"Phantom Pantoum": On average, a person's skin has forty-five miles of nerves.

Talkeetna mountaineer and guide Willi Prittie described Denali in January as "a sufferfest," as cited by the *Huffington Post* and elsewhere. This reference was to a different incident and time of year but seems nonetheless to apply to the 1967 Wilcox Expedition.

"Theories of Flow": The theory about yawning is from a study led by Andrew Gallup, a postdoctoral research associate at Princeton University's Department of Ecology and Evolutionary Biology and coauthor Omar Eldakar, postdoctoral fellow at the University of Arizona's Center for Insect Science. The study was published in May 2013 in the journal *Frontiers in Evolutionary Neuroscience.*

"Hover": The definition of *whiteout* is from Google definitions.

"Ten Variations on a Weight-Bearing Air": The word *circumspangled* was pointed out to me by David Gilbey and comes from Robert Herrick's poem "to His Faithful Friend, M. John Crofts, Cup-Bearer to the King," in *The Hesperides and Noble Numbers.* 2 vols. (London: Lawrence and Bullen, 1898).

The definitions of *algebra* come from (in the order they appear): *Collins English Dictionary: Complete and Unabridged* (New York: HarperCollins Publishers, 2003), *Little Oxford Dictionary of Word Origins* edited by Julia Cresswell, (New York: Oxford University Press 2014), and http://www.etymonline.com/index .php?term=algebra.

"Uncalculable": The Transitive Property of Inequalities can be stated as: If a > b and b > c, then a > c.

"Quaking Aspen": Right-flushed lines are from Isaiah 52:7–9.

"Like Any History, a Family History Repeats": The story from the Ten'a tribe is recounted in (among other places) Brad Olsen's *Sacred Places, North America: 108 Destinations* (San Francisco: CCC Publishing, 2008), 132.

"The Beginner's Guide to Endings": "The chief endeavor of the mind is the endeavor to affirm the existence of the body" is from Spinoza's *The Ethics* and is slightly condensed here.

"Nocturne with Inertia": "Winter is by far the oldest of the seasons" is from Gaston Bachelard's *The Poetics of Space*, trans. Maria Jolas (1958; repr., Boston: Beacon Press, 1994).

"Heresy": Italicized lines in the second to last stanza are from Genesis 32:26.

"Madonna and Particle Child : My Grandfather Outlives His Son": The italicized lines are the ten categories from Aristotle's *Categories*. Wording is borrowed from Wikipedia, http://en.wikipedia.org/wiki/Categories_(Aristotle), accessed on March 31, 2014.

The first part of the title of the poem and lines not italicized are the titles of paintings by Salvador Dali.

About the formal choices: Aristotle's *Categories*, because they were covered in the philosophy book my uncle had asked his parents for (and received) as a college graduation gift. Dali, because my grandfather improbably loved his work.

"Uncertainty Principle": The mountain that had been recognized since 1896 by the US government as Mount McKinley had one of its original Native names, Denali, recognized as its official name by President Barack Obama in August 2015 to agree with the Alaska Board of Geographic Names, which had made the same official gesture in 1975. The meaning of Denali is cited by linguist James Kari in *Shem Pete's Alaska: The Territory of the Upper Cook Inlet Dena'ina* by James Kari and James Fall (Fairbanks: University of Alaska Press, 2003).

Information about the *kakazotsi fantata* comes from "Our Far-Flung Correspondents (Madagascar)," by Alex Shoumatoff, *New Yorker*, March 7, 1988, 62.

"Talkeetna": The historic town of Talkeetna, Alaska, is the base for expeditions to Denali, which are required to register at the Walter Harper Talkeetna Ranger Station to receive climbing permits and orientation. The town cemetery is home to the Mountain Climber Memorial described in the poem.

"American Dusk": "Matter tells space how to curve; space tells matter how to move" is a popular simplification of the quotation "Spacetime tells matter how to move; matter tells spacetime how to curve," which comes from John Archibald Wheeler, *Geons, Black Holes, and Quantum Foam: A Life in Physics*. With Kenneth Ford. (New York: W. W. Norton, 1998) 235.

Since 2002, dozens of accomplished artists, writers, and composers have participated in the Artist-in-Residence program at Denali National Park and Preserve, Alaska. The program includes a ten-day residency, a public outreach activity, and donation of a piece of finished artwork to the program collection.

My residency was an incredibly generous gift from the park service. Being there where my uncle spent his last days was integral to writing this book. Entering the park, I was keenly aware that my uncle had driven the same road, one way. I wandered the Wonder Lake Campground where he had camped and hiked to the banks of the McKinley River, where he had crossed. I hiked as close to the Muldrow Glacier as I could get. I was able to speak to climbers who'd made the same climb by the same route as my uncle had. For an incredible nine days during my visit, Denali was visible; I saw it from many angles and in different weather and at all hours of the day and night. All of these experiences deepened my connection to my uncle and helped me find some peace with my family's story, all the while layering rampant beauty over our profound grief.

JESSICA GOODFELLOW was a writer-in-residence at Denali National Park and Preserve where she researched this project based on the tragic 1967 Wilcox Expedition to Denali, of which her uncle was a member. Her earlier books are *Mendeleev's Mandala* and *The Insomniac's Weather Report*.

Goodfellow's poetry has been featured by *Motionpoems*, *Best New Poets*, and *The Writer's Almanac*. She works at a university in Japan, and imagery from that culture can be found in her writing.